T0113885

REVEREND WITHOUT REVERENCE

A Danger to the Kingdom of God

REV. MARCO SANTOS

WESTBOW
PRESS®
A DIVISION OF THOMAS NELSON
& ZONDERVAN

WestBow Press books may be ordered through booksellers or by contacting:

WestBow Press
A Division of Thomas Nelson & Zondervan
1663 Liberty Drive
Bloomington, IN 47403
www.westbowpress.com
844-714-3454

ISBN: 978-1-6642-8821-8 (sc)
ISBN: 978-1-6642-8820-1 (e)

Print information available on the last page.

WestBow Press rev. date: 12/27/2022

CONTENTS

DEDICATION

I dedicate this small book to the memory of my parents, whom, without any doubt, were the most influential people in my life. Since I was a young boy, they taught me the Holy Scriptures and showed me how to live.

The memories of the services at home with the family, of the nights they spent kneeled in prayer, and of the gatherings with friends on the porch of my grandparents' house, bring to my heart a profound gratitude to God for permitting me to witness the example of a consecrated life before God. I am still filled with emotion when I hear certain hymns from the hymnal "The Warriors prepare for the great fight", number 212, was my father's favorite, and my mother's favorite was "If through the valleys, I, a pilgrim, shall walk", number 515. I can still close my eyes and hear their voices singing and praying.

Many times, as I arrived at home late at night, I heard my parents' payers for my life, asking God to protect me from evil. I am very thankful for those prayers, though they are no longer alive to personally receive my thanks. And though the longing to see them burns in my chest, I know they are in Glory with the Lord and soon I will see them again.

PREFACE

Nothing comes easy in life. One day we are at the top of the mountain and another we find ourselves in a deep valley. There are moments we feel like superheroes and other moments we feel like a rug, trampled by others.

It is for these two types of people that I write this book. My desire is that you understand that the love of God covers you in every circumstance of your life. The Bible tells us that God loved us since before the foundation of the Earth. He has already been in your past, He will be in your future, and He is not surprised by what you are going through today.

Therefore, lift your head, dry your tears, and begin to sing again because winter has passed, in the powerful name of Jesus. We are more than conquerors through the blood shed on the Cross at Calvary.

I also thank God for my wife who challenged me to write this book. After considering many topics, I decided to share with the reader my life and my heart on these pages. My desire is that you would not fall into a sinful, vicious, and profound hole that only brings spiritual defeat.

May God bless you
Marco Santos

1

LIFE IS LIKE A WIND

"As you do not know what is the way of the wind, Or how the bones grow in the womb of her who is with child, So you do not know the works of God who makes everything." Ecclesiastes 11:5 NKJV

Life passes quickly. It is like the breeze that blows from a hurricane, slowly moving the leaves, then little by little increasing in speed until it blows hard enough to knock down giant trees and wipe away everything that is not strongly rooted to the ground. Just when it seems like the hurricane is not going to stop and that everything will be destroyed, little by little the winds slow down, until the calm arrives.

This too is how life is. When we are born, we are defenseless babies, unable to do anything for ourselves. Over time, we learn to crawl, then walk and stand and take our first steps until we gain enough strength in our legs to run like the wind. At this stage it seems as though we are invincible and that we will live forever. But the years go by, and now, the same legs that ran after a soccer ball for hours without tiring, are fatigued and can barely support its own body. At last, what remains is the desire to move in our minds because that hurricane we used to be is about to rest forever. Then we will be remembered by some who knew us such as our spouse, children, parents and friends. They will remember us for the good or bad things we did in our lives.

I personally experienced hurricane Wilma in 2005 and the only thing I remember is spending two weeks without electricity and water. It was unbearably hot in South Florida, but with the passing of time, we forget. We were also visited by hurricane Irma that caused vast damage in the west part of the same state. Now, ask me what is my recollection of this hurricane? I can only remember the inconvenience of having to leave where I lived for a safer place. Irma wreaked havoc elsewhere in the state of Florida, but I personally was unaffected. As I said before, we will be remembered by the things we do in this life, be them good or bad. It may be for this reason that Psalm 90:12 NKJV says, "teach us to number our days, That we may gain a heart of wisdom."

The expression "number our days" does not refer to the amount of dollars we earn in a day, how many joys we have had, what our favorite entertainment has been, or how many sermons we have preached (in the case of preachers). To "number our days" has to do with when we were hurricanes, and we left a legacy that will be remembered as positive accomplishments in life.

Today you may feel indestructible and think you will blow forever. Do you know why hurricane winds often lose strength? The encounter with an obstacle, such as a mountain or tall building, causes its strength to buckle. It is the same with us when we are walking at full speed and suddenly, something crosses our path, weakening our spiritual strength, causing us to lose everything and everyone that was important to us.

I do not think I will be famous for writing this book, and, in fact, this is not my intention. But the purpose of it is for you to review your effort and be wise, not with your own wisdom, but with the wisdom of God, the Almighty. What will your legacy be?

When we believe that we know everything and close our ears to the wisdom of the Word of God, without a doubt, we lose the direction of the path that God has laid out for us. There is a song that we sang years ago that says "Show Jehovah Your ways. Teach me to walk in your paths because I'm tired of mine and I don't want to make any more mistakes". If today someone wants to know my opinion about forging and opening paths for themselves, I tell you that it is the greatest foolish ness in the world that human beings can commit.

I will tell you what happened to me: financial stumbling, personal injury, murder of character, distance from those who claimed to be my friends and even the loss of family affection.

It is not worth it to abandon your house and ministry; it is not worth it to fall for the illusion that someone will make you happy forever, for this is a diabolical lie, a satanic illusion that will give you a short time of pleasure but will rob you of your sleep and dreams of serving God.

The Apostle Paul says, in Galatians 6:17: NKJV "From now on let no one trouble me, for I bear in my body the marks of the Lord Jesus." Unfortunately, I cannot say the same because the marks I have today are of a past of rebellion to the Lord and His Word. Even though it has been a long time, I still live with people who remind me of my past to hurt me.

I am not fortunate enough to say that I have never hurt anyone with deeds or words, and that I have always been a saint and good. I can never say that I have not sinned against the heavens, the Lord's church and my family, but I can say that God has forgiven me and the church (some) have as well. However, I am still discriminated against by others because I got divorced and renounced my credentials in a particular organization. But it happened that when I returned home, the Father removed the dirty rags of sin off me and gave me new clothes and shoes. That is why, for me, there is no problem knowing that there are still people who knew me in the past that have difficulty in valuing what God has given me in the ministry. I continue to believe in Him who called me. He will make me perfect for that Great Day, so that I can present myself before the Father without any guilt of sin.

Once, while traveling to the state of Georgia in southern United States, I heard an African American preacher say that the only one who seeks our sins at the bottom of the sea is the devil, to remind us of our past and make us feel guilty once again. For Jesus has already cast our sins into the deep sea of forgetfulness, never to be remembered again. But that doesn't please the devil and, unfortunately, it doesn't please some people either.

I believe in this truth and no one will change my mind. If it weren't for Him, maybe I would be doing other things out there, but thank God, who, by His Word, tells me that even if my sins are red as scarlet, the blood of Jesus Christ cleanses me from all. sin. That is why I can be sure that my name was written in the book of life. Hallelujah!

Not all people forgive you and forget your past. Maybe that was the reason that when Jesus healed the sick he would say: "your sins are forgiven". Forgiveness brings physical and emotional healing and it removes the burden that was on your shoulders which provides you with the necessary relief to feel free. For this reason, many who accept Christ as their Savior change their countenance and put a smile on their face, because the power of forgiveness is liberating.

There is nothing more devastating than carrying hate in your heart. The Apostle Paul wrote in his first letter to the Corinthians, in chapter 11, an exhortation to the church to examine itself before participating in the Lord's Supper. The sin of hatred, bitterness, jealousy, is as strong or as heavy as the sin of adultery, theft, murder, homosexuality, etc. The only difference between them is that the first is internal, and it may be that no one sees, and the second is external, so everyone can see and comment, so they are more criticized.

But there are some "saints" out there who have never physically committed adultery but have already committed it in thought with thousands of women. The latter must repent in the same way because Jesus said that looking at a woman with carnal desires is the same as having slept with her.

I am not justifying the act of adultery but rather commenting on what the Lord Jesus admonished us. The difference between the two is that while one was physically committed, the other hid in the heart of man, that is, in his thoughts (where he can delight in the wee hours of the morning), often at the same time he has sexual relations with his wife. In fact,

Jesus did not make it easy for anyone when he made this comparison between the Law of Moses and His teachings. The Law said that sin was when a man committed a sexual act with someone who was not his wife (or vice versa). But Jesus went further in this concept and said that anyone who looked at a woman with evil intentions, if not her spouse, was already characterized sinful.

How many people sit in their offices to judge, point fingers and weigh the lives of others when they themselves are far from being those who have no sin. According to the words of Jesus: "He who is without sin among you, let him throw a stone at her first." (John 8:7 NKJV).

I believe in institutions, and I believe that each one has the right to judge, according to its statutes and biblical teachings, the mistakes made by its members. However, they should be less arrogant, remembering what the Apostle Paul warned us: "Therefore let him who thinks he stands take heed lest he fall." (1 Cor. 10:12 NKJV).

Falling is not a difficult task. We are all in risk of stumbling and losing our balance. According to Matthew 7:14, "small is the gate and narrow the road that leads to life, and only a few find it." Our humanistic desire is to please ourselves, making us lose the spiritual path and stopping us from working hard to walk in holiness. Then, little by little, we cool our enthusiasm in wanting to please God.

Those who believe that once we are saved, we are always saved and that from the moment they accept Jesus as their savior, or when they are baptized in water, they are already on their way to heaven and can act as they please for Christ loves them as they are, forget what the Bible says in Hebrews 12:14: NKJV "without holiness no one will see the Lord". This holds true for fornicators, adulterers, the envious, and slanders and all other sinners who, if they do not repent, according to Jesus and the Bible, will go to the lake of fire.

In the countries of the Americas, we see many people in ministries who live in fornication. They go to church but are not asked by their pastors whether they are married under the country's civil laws. Then, they are placed on the altar to minister, without even being right with God. If they are good at giving their tithes, they will go to hell with the complacency of their pastor or wage earner (name by which the pastor who does not care for souls is called).

There are countries that are giving women the legal right to live with a man for a while, without having to marry. Concubinage is the most used word for this. There is no longer an incentive to marry unless they have a desire to serve the Lord. I met many people who said "my husband" or "my wife" not to say "my concubine" or "my concubine". Sounds strong? But this is biblical, and God will not change His word because you do not want to obey. If you live in this situation, ask God for forgiveness, repent and legalize your relationship so as not to lose your soul.

2

HUMBLE CHILD

"God chose the lowly things of this world and the despised things—and the things that are not—to nullify the things that are" 1 Corinthians 1:28 NKJV

I am not ashamed of my humble roots. I was born in southern Brazil, the oldest of five brothers. I grew up in a church pew where the one that governs the boy is Sunday School in the Assemblies of God of Brazil. I have, even today, several memories of when I was a boy and of so many beautiful things I've lived. My father was a great example, not only for me but for many others, of faithfulness to God and others. However, what I would like to share with you is not only the extraordinary story of my parents but about a hurricane that blew in our country in 1954.

All hurricane storms have a name and a specific number, or they may be a less severe storm known as a tropical storm. These are more common and do not have the same intensities as a hurricane.

A tropical storm does not leave structural changes through which they pass, as a hurricane does. In Florida, where I live, two months after hurricane Irma, the city was still being cleared from the rubble of the fallen trees, poles, and electrical wires.

The landscape changes after a hurricane: what was green and, apparently strong, is now on the ground. So, the city's workers need to clean streets, cut down fallen trees, and put them in a truck to make firewood or burn them. The appearances of those trees were superficial, with no root deep in the earth. Therefore, appearance is nothing to be proud of it. Many people are similar to these trees, living in appearance, trying to show off something they are not until the wind called a hurricane comes through their lives and they cannot resist the impact. Soon, they fall apart terribly.

For all babies, milk is essential, especially the maternal milk. When I was a baby, my mother could not breastfeed me, and no other dairy fit me well. One day, she kneeled and cried out to the Lord, "What shall I do?" She then heard a voice that said, "Give him coffee with milk." My mother obeyed and from that moment on, began my first breaths of life. I'm telling this story so that you can see that the "hurricane" started from nowhere.

The Psalmist tells us in Psalm 139:15, *"My frame was not hidden from you when I was made in the secret place, when I was woven together in the depths of the earth."* It was in intimacy that your parents had sexual intercourse, but it was God who gave you existence, formed your bones, and chose the color of your skin. God has perfected you with a purpose, to glorify His name.

You who are reading these lines today, I want you to understand that God has brought you into this world with a purpose. It doesn't matter which part of the world you were born in or what your surname is. If you were born with a golden spoon in your mouth or in the humblest neighborhood of your country - God hopes to make you a powerful instrument in His hands.

> *"Your eyes saw my substance, being yet unformed. And in Your book, they all were written, the days fashioned for me, when as yet there were none of them."*
> Psalm 139:16 NKJV

In God's book, you already existed before you were born. He had already written your story, from the beginning to the end. And the only one able to change your final destination is you. The purpose in our Heavenly Father bringing us to this earth is so that our lives may give glory and honor to His Name through our Testimony.

Some wonder why they were born in a place or situation. But not even you, or your parents, have to do with it. For you had already been planned by the Eternal Father, even before your earthly parents met. Therefore, a thousand questions may arise, such as why this or that, but they will never have answers, for it is the mystery of God. And He didn't make you a robot. Instead, he delegated control of your life to you, giving you the right to choose the end of your soul, which is eternal. When the Psalmist says, your eyes saw my substance, it means that we leave the heavens and return to heaven to spend all eternity with the Lord.

I remember sitting in a wooden pew, in a humble congregation that Dad cared for in southern Brazil, when I heard a Canadian missionary telling us about the snow and how cold it was in North America. I will never forget what happened in my little mind in that moment, I thought, "How beautiful this is! But I'm never going to leave this place where I live."

It seemed impossible for a poor and resourceless boy to consider leaving the edge of his neighborhood. I'm not scientific, and I don't know how hurricanes start, but I think it has to do with some elements in the air that are beginning to consolidate and with the atmospheric pressure taking a direction, forming what we know as a storm or hurricane. That's all of us. To be people who make the difference anywhere in the world, first, we must begin with the elements that surround us, for they will give the direction we should follow.

For example, my parents, more than any other people, influenced me to serve and love God over all things. My father was very dedicated. He took care of a small church that he was in charge of and also had to work secularly as a baker (the pastor in charge, at this time, had no salary). His daily routine was to get up at four in the morning, walk several miles to reach the bus stop, work eight to ten hours and return to the house in the afternoon where he gathered his family around the table to do a devotional service before we left for worship at our church, which began at eight o'clock in the evening.

In Brazil, at the time, almost every night there were activities in the churches. And if you were in charge, you couldn't stay at home. We would walk several kilometers to go and come back. We didn't have a car and I don't remember anyone from church having any vehicle other than a bicycle. But neither rain nor wind were impediments to going to church. There could have been paths of clay along the way and mud on our feet, but it was impossible not to go to God's house.

Those that positively or negatively influence you are the people closest to you. I've never heard my parents speak ill of other brothers and sisters or that it was not worth going to God's house. At no time did they let us stay at home during the time of service. Dedication and love for God's work have always manifested in the life of my parents, who not only spoke of God's love, but they practiced this love.

For my father, the most important thing was the things of the Lord. Continually, he prayed on his knees for hours. That was the solution to any problem. My only visit to the doctor was when I was a teenager when my father was working. Apart from this episode, all diseases were cured by the power of prayer.

I was between five or six years old when I started singing in the local church. One of the church brothers had a radio show and would take me to sing acapella. And it was so that a small, unknown cyclone began to take shape.

I was proud as one of the singers of this program on Farroupilha radio. Then I started singing on Union radio, Come *to Me the Little Ones, and Singing to Jesus*. A long time later, I was the church's soloist in the headquarters of the Assemblies of God (Rua General Neto, 384, Porto Alegre, Rio Grande Sul, Brazil).

How many beautiful memories have I had to have walked with pastors, particularly

Missionary Niles Taranger, who took me to the churches of the rural cities of the State of Rio Grande do Sul. When visiting churches, he played the accordion, and I sang hymns, The poor Blind, etc. There's a chorus that says, "Tell me who you are hanging out with, and I'll tell you who you are." And I could think of being nothing but a preacher of the Word of God.

> *"See, I have this day set you over the nations and over the kingdoms, To root out and to pull down, To destroy and to throw down, To build and to plant."*
> *Jeremiah 1:10 NKJV*

1. Pluck: the evil that was like a wild plant within the hearts of the Jews, who for many years were mistreated in Egypt and brought in their hearts, roots of bitterness, hatred, and contempt. Israel was still a slave in its mind due to memories of the past. Because it is not easy to forget, only the Holy Spirit can tear from the human heart the words and gestures that have hurt us in the past and that today hurt our souls. If every time you remember your past tears fall from your eyes, it's because your soul is wounded. These memories are hidden in your subconscious and only come to light when mentioned again. No Psychologist can erase the pain of your soul or your past. Only the blood of Jesus Christ through forgiveness (He has forgiven us, and we, while offended, must forgive our offenders).

2. Destroy: the myths and complexes that still drag thoughts of inferiority, such as: "I am less than so-and-so," "I am not qualified enough, so I cannot," "I do not deserve," among others—It is the enemy of our souls who wants to keep our minds enslaved. Don't let those thoughts remain in your mind. You are the one who has command of the control tower of your mind, so you can drive out these evil thoughts and send them back to hell, by the name of Jesus.

3. Ruin: satanic works that want to possess the minds of men and women who do not have the full knowledge of the power of God that can make them truly free. One way to ruin the devil's scheme is not to give way to it in your mind. You are more than a conqueror in Christ Jesus. In the course of you being able to bring down satanic works, you have to be stopped, parked, and this may not be a good thing. For example, take a standing tree. If it does not bear fruit, it is of no use. Jesus once stood under a fig tree and sought its fruits but found nothing and thus he cursed it. So, take down from your shoulders all the guilt of the sin that is upon you, and be violent in this. Don't walk through life anymore blaming yourself for past sins. Today will be the day of your victory.

4. Build: once the old building is on the floor and the ground is clear of the rubble, then you can start thinking about building another building in the same place. But

first, the land must be cleared up of what is shattered. We cannot build on ruins. The Bible tells us an old cloth should not be patched up. Therefore, you must first overthrow all the carnal fortresses in your life, the very ones you yourself allowed to rise in your life: pornography, masturbation, and all extramarital delights. Take possession of the authority God gave you to be free, and then begin to build your life as God wants.

5. Planting: due to the conditions of the hearts of the Israelites at the time, a great harvest of love from a loving father who was ready to give a new opportunity to this beloved nation was necessary. It was for this reason that God raised Jeremiah. I do not know much about planting, but I know that it is necessary to clean the land before planting anything and prepare it to cast the seed, otherwise, the seed can die amid the stones and rubble. Let us cultivate the grain of love, truth, peace, service to God and others, respect for others, holiness, and mercy. See how many seeds we can plant! So, cleanse your land so that it bears much fruit—May the Holy Spirit water your heart every day.

I want to emphasize the cleaning of the earth, because this must have a place in the life of a Christian. The seeds are always cast: we ought to allow the good ones to fall deep into the soil of our hearts, but the seeds of gossip, hatred, or bitterness, we ought to yank immediately out, and do so violently. There are people who die carrying a great weight of pain and hurts, mortifying their nerves with sadness and hatred.

The Apostle Peter once asked Jesus how many times we should forgive. I imagine that Jesus' answer surprised Peter and the others who were there. Until that moment, it was taught that it was "an eye for an eye" and "tooth for a tooth," that is, "I slap you, and you have the right to g slap me back." But Jesus said, "Forgive seventy times seven." It's not that easy now.

When I was a pastor, I remember a sister came to my pastoral office to tell me about her husband who mistreated her with blows and words - he was an abuser and torturer. "I'm tired, " she said, "of so much mistreatment. Almost every night, he comes home drunk. What am I supposed to do?" Immediately, what came to my mind was to get a piece of heavy wood for her to put behind the door of her room, so when he assaulted her, she could do the same: hit his head and put him to sleep. So next time, he would think better before he assaulted her.

It is not easy to forgive an abusive person who humiliates you repeatedly without worrying that it can damage your spirit and emotional life. That's why so many end up taking their own lives.

Once, someone who was going through this kind of situation told me that usually people who abuse others are abusive because they have also suffered some abuse in their life. It's like a satanic current. The only way to break this is through forgiveness. A person abused needs to forgive his or her aggressor so that the wound is healed and so that the person has no sense of revenge in their mind or heart.

You can say, "It's not fair what happened." And I agree with you because it should never have happened to you – not to you or anyone else. Satan used someone to make another innocent also suffer. It's not fair to act the same way.

My advice to those reading this book that have suffered abuse in the past is to seek emotional help. Get out of this hiding place that you created to hide your pain. Breathe the air of freedom, run like an innocent child, without any care and fear, and seek the arms of the eternal Father because He has never hurt you.

I didn't want to accept that a father or mother allowed something terrible to happen to their children. But when someone does not fear God in their life, they can do anything to those who are most vulnerable.

Right now, I have an incredible frustration when I see what goes on with the elderly and children of the country where I live due to the financial crisis and social injustice. Not a day goes by when my wife and I don't come across hungry and thirsty people. However, in many restaurants, we are forbidden to feed them due to their appearance.

Many people are resentful of those who have a higher social position, but many do not recognize that it is not to accumulate but rather share with those in need. In addition, there is a generation of children and young people who grow up and think that everything in life comes easy - it's easier to kill and steal to get what I didn't get by my sweat. We have lost the values of human coexistence, and we can only ask God to keep our children and grandchildren. I don't know how many more years of life God will give me, but I pray and wonder what the future of our descendants will be if God does not intervene in humans once more. In the Old Testament, as things reached a level that God could no longer tolerate, then, He sent fire and brimstone to Nineveh and Gomorrah and destroyed them for so much sin. How much more will God accept in our day? The millions of abortions? Homosexuality? The open practice of Satanism? The indifference of governments to the people? The injustices, evils, and discrimination of races? Among other things.

And what can we say about our churches? Idolatry of preachers and singers, immorality, vulgarity, the false doctrine of prosperity, and the use of the Lord's name in vain. Also, adultery, formication, cynicism, lack of forgiveness, and lack of love for others.

I wonder how much more God will tolerate before we are consumed. We know that He is merciful and long-suffering, but the Bible tells us that He is also a consuming fire. I believe God will visit us.

3

THE CALLING

"He said to them, 'Go into all the world and preach the gospel·to every creature."
Mark 16:15 NKJV

What is our call? In Brazil, almost all boys love soccer, and I was no exception. In those years, sports were considered a sin by evangelical churches – especially soccer. In my church, there was even a sister who accused me all the time of kicking the "devil's head."

But when we were not playing soccer, my brothers and I, along with some of the neighbors' children, played church. Many of these children were sons and daughters of our church brothers. One afternoon the Holy Ghost baptized us with fire and many of us began to speak in tongues in that place. I was about seven or eight years old and many were even younger. Now, it was no longer a joke, but the fire of the Spirit that blew upon us, to uproot the evils of the enemy. Next to our humble house lived a lady who made healings through the batuque (macumba). Usually, in the afternoon, people were starting to come from everywhere to get healing from her.

However, as the children began to sing and worship God, the lady's demons could not act, and she had to send all the people back to their homes. As a justification, she said that the air was closed and no saint could help. The power of God was coming down upon us, and the fresh breeze of the Holy Spirit blew to cancel all evil work. No matter our age, the important thing was that we were God's instruments in that place. In fact, we did not worship to bother the neighbor, but where there is the light of Christ, the power of darkness cannot stand.

Jeremiah 1:9 NKJV says, Then the Lord put forth His hand and touched my mouth, and the Lord said to me: "Behold, I have put My words in your mouth."

What God requires of us is that we rise to uproot the devil's lies with our words. We can see how false doctrines grow like a big, strong tree whose leaves are green and beautiful, but their fruits are poisonous. All it takes is a small bite of these fruits to start feeling superior to others (pride), thinking: "No one does anything like me," "There is no one who sings as beautiful as Me," etc. Satisfaction is where we put ourselves at the center of everything. A proud person is arrogant and pretentious, often false with the other and herself, for lack of security.

After Hurricane Irma, one of the things I noticed was the number of giant trees uprooted. If by chance, you had stopped under its shadow the day before the hurricane and walked its monstrous trunk, contemplating its beauty and the sounds of the leaves that made a beautiful song as it rose from the wind, you would say that this tree would last for many years. But you didn't know that its roots were shallow and never entered the depth of the earth, so it couldn't stand the breath of the wind. This is how some people are: they look powerful, but they hide behind security barriers that prevent our access to them.

A while back, I went to preach at a large church and before the service began, I told the pastor I needed to go to the bathroom. The pastor called four escorts to accompany me. On the way to the bathroom, it was necessary to go through the entrance where people were arriving through for service. I could not salute them. A friend of my wife's wanted to greet me, but she was stopped.

Unfortunately, this shows that we look like Hollywood actors, where pastors no longer want to be called pastors and are outraged when someone calls them such.

Jesus, being the Shepherd of all shepherds, did not change his title but said, "I am the good shepherd and I give my life for my sheep." The prophet Jeremiah had a commitment to be called a trumpet that had sounded the truth of God's word, also known as the weeping prophet. It is with tears that we let go of the word to uprooted sin and evil. Therefore, those who preach without feeling and without feeling mercy for those who have been lost are not the mouth of God because compassion and mercy are synonymous to God who has loved us since the consummation of time.

A while back, I heard a pastor proudly say that he had no compassion, no mercy. He confessed that he could verbally assault without any remorse. However, when it is necessary to correct, a faithful pastor must have the heart of a father; if not, the people lose respect and affection for him.

"The priests did not say, where is the LORD? And those who handle the law did not know Me; The rulers also transgressed against Me; the prophets prophesied by Baal, And walked after things that do not profit" Jeremiah 2:8 NKJV

The husband, the father of the family, is the priest of his house. According to Jeremiah, God's complaint was to the priests — all those who lead a home. We cannot fail to exercise our ministry. We should teach our children the word of God — this is not just a Sunday Bible School teacher's task.

When someone would ask my father what he intended to do in the future, his answer was always, "If God wants, I will do" But when the family priest assumes that he is in total control, without considering God's will, that is where the collapse of his home begins. Joshua marked the territorial lines of his house and began his discourse with these words: "And if it seems evil to you to serve the Lord, choose for yourselves this day whom you will serve" Joshua 24:15 NKJV As the authority of his house, Joshua went on to say that he had already made his decision: "I and my house shall serve the LORD." Joshua, as the authority of his home was saying that he had made his decision: "As for me and my house, we will serve the Lord" The decision is undoubtedly an individual one. You don't force any person to be a Christian. How many children of shepherds do we see today that do not serve the God of their fathers?

Joshua continued his speech, asking a question: "If the gods your fathers served were not real, what did you continue after them?" When I pastored a church in the Andes of Venezuela, I decided to do a research with the young University students of the church. They went from house to house, without the Bible in their hands, doing a brief interview, and one of the many questions asked was: "What is your religion? And why is that?" The result was that more than 80% claimed to be Roman Catholic. Another question was, "Why do you belong to this faith?" Without thinking twice, everyone said it was because of the influence of their parents or grandparents. These showed that most had no personal conviction of their belief. I believe that if we still asked what these gods did for them, they would undoubtedly answer, "Nothing!" Because they were other people's gods. The God of our fathers is no good to us if we do not make him our God.

I remember when I was a 14-year-old and we arrived in the city of Chicago to live there. I had a very high ego because, in Brazil I had fans since I was known singer in the churches of southern Brazil. I participated in radio programs and considered myself popular.

The church in Chicago only had about fifty people, between Ukrainians and Brazilians. In the first few months, I sang in all the services, but as time went by, I lost the desire to go to church, for I began to tire of the same physiognomies as always. Besides, I didn't give any more autographs nor hear compliments such as: "You sing so well." But on a Saturday night, during a period of prayer, I had to make my own decision: all this time, did I served the Lord out of love or for having the applause of the audience.

It draws my attention to the story of when Elisha returned from the other side of the river where he had met with Elijah. Elisha lifts Elijah's robe and cries out to the God of Elijah and the waters opened. I can't tell if Elisha did not have faith that the God of Elijah was also his God. The God of Elijah had already opened the sea once, but this was the last time Elisha mentioned God as "the God of Elijah." From this moment on, he had Jehovah as his God.

We cannot walk with God if we do not make him our God. The God of our grandparents or our parents does not serve us if we do not have Him as ours. The Apostle John says that to all who believe in the name of Jesus, He has given the authority to be called children of God. Children have the identity of their father. They also know their father and are known by him. It is intimate living with the father that makes us blessed and happy children.

When I have a need, I seek my God, the savior of my life. It is He to whom I cry out to as a son, and He answers me as the kind Father He is. It is not necessary to twist the arm of the heavenly Father so that He will bless us, nor send money to any pastor to receive our healing, or for a spouse to return home, or for a child to be free of drugs, for He does not sell his blessing. What He expects of us is obedience and faith in Him to respond to our petitions.

Preachers are called to open the eyes of our faith. The moment our spiritual eyes open, then the passion for the Lord begins. In the church, there are many who are convinced that Jesus is the Lord but, are not in love with Him. It is the passion that leads you to have intimacy, and it is intimacy that brings pleasure and satisfaction, to the point that the closer we get to Him, the more we will want to walk together.

There are people who think about God only on Sundays. They go to their Beloved's house for just a few minutes to thank for life, or ask for the whole week, because for the rest of the week they never mention God's name nor do they remember that He exists unless something bad happens.

In a church where I pastored, there was a young man who seemed to be very dedicated to God and prayer. He went to morning prayer every day. His mother, on the other hand, wanted nothing to do with the Gospel and spoke ill of all the pastors she knew. One morning, she called me, troubled, because her son wanted to jump off the balcony of his apartment to commit suicide. Not knowing what to do, she said she had thought of God and remembered me, so she decided to look for me.

God, church, and pastors, for many, are like death rescue boards – they are only thought of in times of affliction and tribulation, but soon are forgotten when everything passes over. Again and again, I was called to this same apartment to pray and rebuke the disturbing spirit that came over this young man whenever he listened to Hard Rock music on his tape recorder that sat beside his bed.

The Bible tells us in 1Peter 5.8 NKJV that the devil walks around us like a roaring lion, seeking whom to devour, and when a son of God opens a window of their soul, that lion enters. But he's not liked the Holy Spirit who knocks on the door of the heart until the person invites him to join. The devil is like a thief, devourer, liar, deceiver, forger of the truth of God, and he waits for a loophole to be opened to enter the person's life.

Satan's intention is to enter your life to give you a short time of pleasure. All he can offer you is temporary: a drink here, a drug there - to make you forget reality - a borrowed bed, an adventure of revenge of the spouse who has deceived you, etc. All these things apparently bring joy. But their duration is, at maximum, until the next morning. When you realize, that drink gave you a headache, the drug burned your neurons, the bed that was not yours made you feel guilty, and revenge did not make you feel better. I never understood what the pleasure is in taking alcoholic drinks and waking with a hangover, for it seems that the pain lasts longer than the enjoyment of the night before.

The sacred scriptures recommend that we should not get drunk with wine, but to be filled with the Holy Spirit, for the Spirit does not bring any malaise to your body or to its conscience. You will rise in the morning with the joy of the Lord, a supernatural joy, with a song on your lips. The psalmist tells us, in Psalms 34.8 KNJV "Taste and see that the Lord is good."

4

A HURRICANE CALLED MARCO

"Therefore, let him who thinks he stands take heed lest he fall" 1 Corinthians
10:12 NKJV

A few years ago, Hurricane Marco was very active in my life: many appointments,
invitations to preach, travel, and so many other distractions. Suddenly, I noticed
that I was losing my spiritual strength, for I no longer prayed sufficiently, I did not
read the Bible regularly, and moreover, a person crossed my path and caused the
wind of the Holy Spirit to go out in my life. God is the same and is powerful to deliver us
from temptation. However, we must seek that freedom and take shelter in it, lest we fall.

Psalmist David says in Psalm 91:1: NKJV " He who dwells in the secret place of the
Highest Shall abide under the shadow of the Almighty."

I have met many people who have this psalm as an amulet, and they keep their Bible
open in this chapter to protect their home or business. In case you are reading this book,
believe it, I will give you bad news: our only shelter is when we take our soul, mind, and
spirit to the shelter. We are solely responsible for being kept from evil, not God. While we
hide in Him, we have Him as the cornerstone, which is immutable and our refuge. If on
the contrary, we are unprotected.

Remember that I mentioned earlier those hurricanes decrease strength when encountering resistance or obstacles, and die ahead of time?

When you take your gaze off Jesus Christ, you become prone to being ambushed by evil spirits of envy, adultery and lies. First of all, envy. You start looking for the largest church in town and then you are taken over by a spirit of discontentment that makes you doubt your calling and place. Envy is sin - so the Bible tells us. But it's because of this little door that spiritual cooling begins. That leads you not to be grateful to God for what He has given you, and not to value what is yours.

If King David was not grateful to God for the few sheep of his father's flock which was under his care, perhaps he would never have reached the place where he arrived. The stage on which he served was the place where Saul's servant could testify of his life, saying to the king, "Bring him to the palace, because he carries something that make a difference in your life, Oh, King."

Secondly, right after envy comes physical and mental adultery, which will cause you to no longer preach about this sin, for it will take away your authority. That's because you'll know that God has the knowledge of your sin and because of your concern about whether anyone in the church hsd seen you enter a hotel with someone other than your wife. The devil is a torturer, and he accuses you and torments you day and night, saying you are going to hell.

I have always believed, and believe, that if a person in adultery does not repent, they will go to the eternal fire that will never go out, as the Bible says. For preaching and listening to so many other messages in that regard, I spent sleepless nights by the effect that this word would bring upon me.

Thirdly, are the lies that are told to cover your bad steps. The person begins by lying to their spouse, their children, their secretary, until they became a first-rate liar to escape and deflect the blame. When I returned to the U.S.A I left the priesthood and ministry and sold car to survive in the city of Miami. My finances had been completely destroyed. I was family-less and spiritually defeated.

He who, a few years ago, had begun as a hurricane - having the financial support of a significant amount of large and small churches across the country - now had lost everything and all. The ones who claimed to be my friends simply abandoned me without wanting to know anything of me -- I stood like a leper.

When I got to Miami, I soon went to look for a church, to attend. It was a small church in number and the pastor was already quite old but would remain there until the church elected someone younger to take his place. After telling the pastor my story, from where I came, what I had done and how much I was truly sorry, he was pleased with me. So he told me that he would like to hear me preach, even though he knew that this could create a serious problem, both for him and for the congregation, because I had been separated by my district. But at a men's breakfast, I got an opportunity.

I had a longing to preach again. So, my pastor friend began to call me to do the final prayer of the service, and I took the opportunity to say some things that I felt. I enjoyed these moments and often came out with tears running down my face, seeing how much I missed the ministry.

I began to return the things that were under my responsibility and that belonged to the mission. I called my missionary colleague, who was in charge of the missionaries, so that he would deliver to the engineer responsible for the construction, an elevator of material that belonged to him. But this brother, did not believed my words, they thought that I wanted to keep to myself the materials that belong to the mission.

When you go out and stop being God's hurricane to destroy the sin of lies and deception, you will end up being annihilated by those who mercilessly see you as the enemy of God. They become the avengers of the faith.

The truth is that dear brothers who never fell into grotesque sins, such as adultery, do not know how we are treated and believe that if they approach us, they will be contaminated by the same leprosy. Let's not talk about the mercy of God that we should demonstrate to all sinners. It is much more difficult to forgive our brothers, so we become judges.

The second part of Jesus' commandment is to love others as yourself. This is also very difficult, because it requires an extraordinary effort on our part. It's easier to feel pity than mercy. So, the only way to love is when we love God over all things.

While I'm writing this book, my wife and I opened a non-profit organization called Mercy & Salvation, where we feed a lot of people, be it the elderly, or children. I suffer from seeing humans suffering, but I know God loves them. However, to have mercy and to feed is not loving. I can give someone a plate of food and not remember that person anymore. But God never forgets them because He loves them. So, what I can do is convey this love through my works.

In the book of St. Luke, Chapter 15, we have three well-known parables, that of the prodigal son being the best known among them. Many often preach about the younger brother who left home to waste dad's money. But there's hardly any talk about the older brother, who remained at home but never sought to know the father's heart. This one suffered every time they ate together, and he saw an empty seat at the table and lost his appetite. Any son who loves his father could see the anguish that transpired from his face. But not this this son.

If we don't learn to see through dad's eyes, we never will learn to discern the father's heart. We can even remain at home, but we will always be ungrateful children. Children who do not care about their father's heart are self-centered, they only think of themselves and care only about their reputations. But the father loves everyone equally, no matter the number of children he has, all are equally important and loved. What the father wants is that his children share with him the joys and pains, embrace him, and say they are with him, that they also suffer from the departure of their brother and pray for him to return home.

Do we think that our brother is our competition and for this reason we do not care that he has left? Or do we think that the fewer people sitting at the table the more leftover food there will be for us? What would be the reason for not seeking the reconciliation of our fallen brothers? It seems that often we are content when a neighboring shepherd falls, because that means more sheep to our flock.

I once heard the following comment: "The only army that kills their own soldiers is God's army." How sad to note that we no longer defend our brothers and sisters. Instead, we offend them and hurt them with words and instead of helping them get up, we push them even further to the abyss.

In my two years out of ministry, only two people who knew me before reached out to me and cheered me up, encouraging me to return to the ministry. How many of us would give King David a chance to be a minister if we only looked at the day of his adultery? Or who would invite Moses to walk beside them upon learning that he had killed a person? But we only remember these characters to talk about when one killed Goliath and the other led the people to the promised land. They became the heroes of their times after they failed. Only God to use two types of people who wouldn't stand a chance with us.

Unfortunately, there is competition between ministers, not only about denomination. They all represent the Kingdom of God, so when someone speaks ill of some other brother, he is diminishing the Kingdom of God.

Denominations have their presidents who watch over their rules and customs, but the One who represents the bride of the lamb is Jesus Christ, the Son of the Highest God, who paid a high price for her. I think that the blood of many will be demanded by God from pastors who mistreated sheep and caused them to flee from the fold and instead of using the staff to lift them they struck them until they lost their strength and died.

In most cases, it was just a broken paw that required a bandage, a thorn in the flesh, or a human weakness. But as we shepherds are almost reaching divine stature, we have just annihilated the sheep that never belonged to us. If you don't believe me, then ask any pastor what the value of a soul is. Perhaps he has evangelized and discipled a sheep, but the price of forgiveness of sins and the hope of eternal life, the pastor cannot buy to give away. Therefore, he offers something that was already bought by Jesus.

The Apostle Paul says that we were bought at the price of blood. At the market we can buy a liter of blood. There are some countries that pay for blood donors, but this blood, before it is used on another person, has to go through a purification process to remove all impurity. But the precious blood of Jesus already has everything that is necessary to cleanse all our sins, for the glory of His Name.

5

THE DESIRE TO SERVE

"But when he came to himself, he said, 'How many of my father's hired servants have bread enough and to spare, and I perish with hunger" Luke 15:17 NKJV

I had a huge desire to return to the ministry but felt like I was in a prison of impossibilities. All my life I had served God in an organization, but now I started looking for other denominations that accepted divorced persons, broken, and disconnected from ecclesiastical organization. However, I have never finished filling out the required paperwork, for I had an internal struggle. Although I know that all organizations serve the same God, the battle in my mind was strong.

One day, finalizing a car sale, I walked into a building to sign the papers, and a large automatic door opened in front of me. At that instant was when I heard, for the first time, the audible voice of God. He said to me, "Go back to the place (country) that you have fallen, and there I will raise you again." Throughout my entire life, I heard the Lord speak to me in spirit, through the word, but this time it was different. I was thrilled! So, I went to the bathroom, bent my knees and I prayed, "Lord, I will do so, as soon as possible."

Two months passed, and I left two cars and a rented apartment with a friend who lived with me. With three bags of clothes and six hundred dollars in my pocket, I returned to the country of my calling.

A friend picked me up at the airport. Without having a set place to go, I told him I would like to go to a certain city because I had heard of a church that was living a great revival there. And how I wanted to do something for God, I thought this might be a good opportunity to help. And this friend of mine, who lives in the State of California, knew the pastor of this church.

The next night, after seven hours by bus, I arrived at my destination. The only time I went to that side of the country was as a Missionary, where I spent two weeks in a luxurious Hotel, to enjoy my vacation. My friend had already contacted the local pastor and sent a very polite young man to pick me up at the bus station. But along the way, he ended up asking me several questions, like, "What did you come to do here? It is not very often that someone comes from Miami to live in this city to serve the Lord here. Who is your covering?" He kept insisting on these and other questions, and I began to get annoyed with so many questions.

Finally, when we arrived at the church, I noticed that it operated in a large shed and didn't look like much of a church. It had a pretty high platform, and lots of chairs that filled the place. Many young people worked on the decoration of the altar and wore personalized shirts, which said: "We are a thousand".

For a while, I was just watching the environment and talking to one person or another. Then the young man who had picked me up at the bus station came to where I was and asked, "Pastor, do you already have a place to sleep? Because I need to take the brothers to their homes, but their suitcases occupy space in the vehicle". My answer was that I didn't have a place to stay and took the opportunity to ask for an indication of some economic hotel close by where I could sleep one night and then look for another place. So, he suggested a little hotel, which was four blocks away from the church, and took me there.

It was a very small and very humble place. It had three rooms that only fit a twin bed, some nails on the walls to hang clothes, an air-conditioning that made a noise like a turbine of an old plane that's running on the runway to take off and some huge mosquitoes that wouldn't let me sleep, besides the tiredness I felt from the trip. I started to doubt that I was doing things the right way. Far from all that luxury which I was accustomed to, I began to question myself wondering if the voice I heard was not my madness or just a desire to return to ministry.

Daylight finally penetrated the small window of the little room, and I got up to bathe and dress to go meet the pastor, who would be at the church after nine o'clock in the morning. When I went into the bathroom, I noticed the shower was a pipe and I needed to be right in the corner to be able to get my head wet, but still only a little cold water fell. I struggled not to think of the five-star hotels of the past, for, now, I was on a mission of true missionaries. I kept telling myself that missionaries have no luxury, to keep hope that something better would happen in my future.

Of the six hundred dollars I brought to the country, I exchanged it with my pastor friend – the same one who picked me up at the airport – since before leaving the Capital, to help him with ministry.

Still, I had set aside a bundle of money that could impress anyone who didn't know about the country's inflation. I took some notes out of my suitcase and left the hotel to buy a coffee and a meat pastry. That's when I started to see where I was, and I realized that I had never walked alone in such a dangerous place before. Being from South America, I wasn't afraid of my appearance, as everyone there is very similar. But my Spanish accent would give me away as a foreigner.

When I worked as a Missionary, I remember having guns pointed at my head seven times in attempted robberies. Those are not very pleasant memories. I am grateful to God for His deliverances, but at that moment I was scared. As I was already in the neighborhood, I couldn't do anything but pray in spirit that God would make me invisible to the bad guys. I also thought about walking steadily, without looking too far to the sides, trying to demonstrate that I dominated that territory, without drawing people's attention too much.

Suddenly, something happened, and I lost track of how to get back to the hotel or how to get to the church. "What can I do?", I thought, "I'll have to open my mouth and say I'm lost. Surely, they will know that I am not from here." On a corner, there was a man selling vegetables. I decided to approach him, and I asked: "Friend, can you please let me know how I get to this church?" Immediately, he replied: "Sir, if you are not from here, it is not recommended to walk alone, because there are many bad people in this place". Honestly, that was the last thing I wanted to hear at that moment. Fear soon returned to my heart.

When I arrived at the church, I was terrified. I rang the bell several times (on weekdays, all the entrances of the church were closed), and within a few minutes someone came to answer me. I identified myself as the missionary who was arriving and wanted to meet the pastor. Supposedly, my friend from California had already told the pastor about me via e-mail, and I had also written to him about my desire to serve the Lord in any part of the ministry.

After several minutes of waiting, the pastor welcomed me into his small but comfortable office. He ordered coffee to be brought to me, and then we began a dialogue between someone who was totally determined to serve the church and the Lord in whatever way possible and a pastor who was suspicious of my desires. He didn't want to understand how I came from the US to serve in this place. He thought I might have some other intention, and so he was suspicious.

On the first Sunday, with the auditorium full, the pastor called me to give a greeting to the church, and these were his words: "He says he is a pastor, but I confess that I am not very sure about this individual". That was the last time I stood in the pulpit of this church. Nine months passed, and I had done everything but the ministry of the word.

At least I got a dirty mattress and a small fan to calm the intense heat that was in that place. I slept next to the pulpit. The moment I turned off the lights in the shed to sleep, the party of rats, cockroaches and all kinds of insects began. But I still wanted to be of useful to the kingdom again. So, every night my thought was, "one day the pastor will see my sincerity and give me a family group to minister to."

One day, I got up very early, because I had to open the church doors for the brothers who came to the morning service, but my body was no longer warm – it was burning with fever and I was in a lot of pain. I dressed as best I could and went to prayer. However, the sisters realized that I was not in good health, so they recommended a church doctor who could help me. Someone gave me a sum of money and directed me to take a blood test at a laboratory near the church.

As I feared, the test result showed dengue. "And now, Lord, what do I do?" - I asked. I didn't have anyone to offer me a glass of water, I didn't have any more money, because it was my mother who deposited twenty dollars a month into my account to help me. On the contrary, for many days my only food was a bowl of soup which the pastor gave me to eat, as he had a restaurant near the church.

I felt like the prodigal son, as it is written: "But when he came to himself, he said, 'How many servants of my father have plenty of bread, and I perish here with hunger!'" Luke 15:17 NKJV. I started to question myself about what I was doing there. "Marco, ask your mother to buy you a ticket back to Miami, and forget about the ministry in this place" – was my daily thought. The situation was very difficult, and I could not share with my dear mother what I was going through, as I didn't want to worry her too much. Every day we talked on the phone, and she prayed for me. There is no prayer more beautiful than a mother's prayer for her child.

Finally, I got better from dengue, but everything remained the same. I had not yet received any opportunities from the pastor, other than to teach English to a small group that met on Saturday afternoons. It gave me the opportunity to buy a candy and a soda every now and then.

One night I dreamt that I was in a country house where there were many trees. Upon entering the main house, I found the pastor on his knees and his wife beside him. He had his arm inside an industrial dryer, and when he noticed that I was approaching, he took out a blanket and said: "Take it and put it on, because this is to cover your nudity". Immediately, I misinterpreted the dream and thought that the blanket symbolized a ministry and that would be the victory I was waiting for. That same morning, I went to him to tell him about the dream. However, all they did when they heard my story was laugh at me, then they would look at each other and laugh again.

One day I got a phone number for a friend who was the director of the Central Institute in this country. I called him, and I told him what was happening in my life, and that I had come back to the country to do something for God, but it didn't work out, and now I was thinking about the possibility of returning to the USA. In response, he told me: "Before returning to your country, stop by and stay for a few days. I'll see what I can do for you." I quickly collected the money for the ticket. It would be a bit of a long journey, as it was twelve hours on the road from where I was.

Upon arriving at Bible school, my friend said, "I already have a church for you to preach at tomorrow. It is the opening of a new temple and the presiding brother who is the official preacher will not be able to arrive in time. Would you be willing to take his place?" I couldn't believe that after almost nine months in the country, I was now being asked to replace the organization's president. My mouth was open, not knowing what to say.

The director said the service would begin at seven o'clock at night. I started to get ready, and I was quite anxious. I couldn't believe this opportunity. I was walking to the entrance to wait by the gate, when I heard a car horn and the voice of a guard saying: "Brother Santos, they came to get you". After about twenty minutes of travel, we arrived at the church. It was a very beautiful and large place, full of people waiting to hear the president of the organization preach. But instead, I, a total stranger, introduced myself as the preacher of the night. The pastor very kindly thanked me for taking the president's place and called me to the pulpit with him.

The service began, and I couldn't believe that I was sitting in a pulpit again, and that I was going to preach to a crowd. If this was a dream, I didn't want anyone to wake me up. I don't remember what I preached about that night, but I do remember making an alter call for those in need to come to the altar and many came. The temple was filled with the glory of God.

At the end of the service, the pastor approached me, placed an envelope in my hand, and said, "Thank you so much for ministering tonight. If you're passing through town at another time, let me know so I can invite you to preach again." Excited, I replied, "Of course, pastor." I was very happy for this opportunity.

Now, I began sleeping in the student dormitory, with a clean bed and a fan. They also offered me three meals a day. I was feeling very happy with God - it was heaven on earth.

It was after three in the afternoon when someone knocked on my dorm door, saying that the director was calling me to his office. Arriving there, he told me that there seemed to be a problem with the president that prevented him from being present. Then he told me that the pastor asked him to ask me if I would be willing to preach all that week. "Of course!", I replied, almost without strength in my legs, from so much emotion. What a joy! It didn't take long for this pastor and I to become friends.

Now, I began to see the door that God had told me about, opening. I stayed in that city for over a month, preaching in different places almost every night. And it was in this place that my Evangelistic ministry began, doors from North to South, from East to West, and to other countries that border. God is Faithful! From then on, I could also understand that the pastor's rejection of me was on God's part. If he had accepted me there, I would never have gone to other places and other nations.

How many times do we think that God is not in our boat, just because things aren't going the way we think they should? We often say that if God were in the matter, it would be different. But the problem is that we only see today, but God has already been in your past, he is in your present and he will also be in your future if you will allow Him.

6
COVERING

So, David said to Nathan, "I have sinned against the Lord." And Nathan said to David, "The Lord also has put away your sin; you shall not die. 2 Samuel 12:13 NKJV

The cover that I had dreamed of was not ministerial, because the pastor never took me into account, but it was my wife (who attended that church). She was a servant and intercessor on the morning prayer team, and one of her occupations was to make breakfast for her pastors and wash the bathroom. He never realized the potential and talent of my wife, who is a prophetess and minister of the word. Even though she rejected me three times, when I approached her to talk about dating, the final time, I won and the pastor ended up doing our wedding ceremony, three months later. He covered my nudity.

One day, I sat under the shadow of a big tree, with a pencil and a notebook in my hand. I was looking for words to write to my family, to the district I had belonged to and to the department to which I was connected formerly, to ask forgiveness for the mistakes made, knowing that I had tarnished the name of Jesus Christ and also their name, as an institution that represents the kingdom. I had failed.

A while later, I went to visit a missionary sister. Surprised, she handed me a letter from the director of the mission department saying that I was forgiven by him and that he was willing to help me get back on my feet in ministry.

A few years later, I had the privilege of being with him in a restaurant in Miami, and again he said the same words to me. The letter he had sent me (I keep it with me to this day) was addressed to Reverend Marco Santos. It's not that I was impressed by the title, but I thought that because I had renounced my credentials and pleaded guilty to my sins, the first thing I would lose would be the title. It reminded me of the father's love, that even after the son had left his home, when he returned, he continued with the same title as son. Even if a child is an alcoholic, drug addict or prostitute, in the father's eyes, he will never stop being a child. To everyone else you may be bad, but to the father you will always be a dear son.

I remember being at a bus station, waiting for the time to board to go towards a city in order to preach. There was an elderly lady, who sat next to me. We struck up a conversation and I asked her what she was going to do in the city she was going to. She told me that she was going to visit her dear son, who was in prison. With conviction, she argued that he was innocent of all the things he was accused of. For a father or a mother, the children will always be innocent.

In fact, we will never know this son's innocence, but I know that when he gets out of prison, he will have a mother who believes in his innocence and opens the doors of her house every time he wants to visit her.

So, is the problem between the brothers? It's not that we have difficulty forgiving and forgetting, but we behave like those that judge who deserves forgiveness and who doesn't; we are the owners of the balance of good and evil, and we weigh the sins of others.

St. Matthew 7:2 NKJV says, "For with the judgment with which you judge, you will be judged, and with the measure you use, it will be measured to you." The Roman Catholic Church uses certain measures for sins to be forgiven, and they say: "You must pray as many Hail Marys as many Our Fathers, that you may be freed from your guilt." But Holy Scripture tells us that our sins are forgiven and blotted out forever, through the blood that Jesus Christ shed on Calvary.

In 1 John 1:7 NKJV it is written, "But if we walk in the light, as he is in the light, we have fellowship with one another, and the blood of Jesus Christ his Son cleanses us from all sin."

Our sins are forgiven and washed away by the blood of Jesus. But then we must walk in the light so that we can have communion with one another as one body. Being cleansed by the blood of Jesus is not difficult or impossible, we just have to accept Jesus as our only and sufficient savior and confess him as Lord. Now, walking in the light is not easy, because it allows our brothers to see the flaws we have, which often shock those who like to comment on the lives of others. Finally, having fellowship with one another is another story. Most people only fellowship with those of their own church, or denomination. So, if they do not belong to our council, we exclude them. We often become ridiculous and hypocritical thinking that God only supports our denomination because women don't wear makeup, or because pastors don't wear beards, etc. If you believe that your salvation is in your physical appearance, I am sorry to inform you that you are wasting your time as a Christian.

King David once said that God does not look on the outside, but at the heart and its intention. My father used to say that it is better to have a short skirt than a wide tongue, because people will be judged by their tongue and not by their dress. I particularly love to change my appearance. For a while I have a beard, other times I clean it, sometimes I let my hair grow a little, other times I keep it short, etc. So for the religious, I'm just considered a Christian depending on how I look. But that doesn't bother me anymore.

When I was pastoring a church in the Andes, one morning after the service ended, a brother approached the altar, identifying himself as a high-ranking member of a denomination. He then invited me to be the preacher of the General Congress that was to be held in that city, and said to me: "Brother, I would love for you to be the official preacher of this festivity, but only if you are willing to cut your beard, because our organization does not accept men with beards". I answered him: "Pastor, what an honor to meet you. I appreciate your invitation, but right now I have no intention of shaving my beard. Later, perhaps, I will and then we can make an appointment."

A week later, that same pastor called me and said, "Brother, we had a meeting and we decided to make an exception for this conference because you are a foreigner." So, I confirmed it and it was two nights of great glory. Many people received the baptism of the Holy Spirit. We saw tremendous manifestations of God, and it seems that my beard was no impediment for God to work.

But someone may ask me, "Wouldn't it be easier to cut the beard for this occasion?" I answer you: Yes and no. Yes, because if I had cut my beard to preach, they would say that my anointing was for not having a beard, and they would say that I was just like everyone else. But since I had a beard, they were able to learn that God works with or without a beard, for He only seeks a circumcised heart to use. It is sad to see how much damage some places of worship have caused for making exception of people by their outward appearance (like the way they dress, for example), when God does not see the outside of man but what is inside the heart.

Dad always said that in heaven we will have many surprises. We will be able to see those people we think are unworthy and sinful, and we may not find those we thought would be there. For God does not have our earthly scales, and his judgment is different from ours.

7

IRREVERENCE

"Then the anger of the Lord was aroused against Uzzah, and God struck him there for his error; and he died there by the ark of God." 2 Samuel 6:7 NKJV

J eremiah 2:8 says, NKJV "The priests did not say, 'Where is the Lord? 'And those who handle the law did not know Me; The rulers also transgressed against Me; The prophets prophesied by Baal And walked after things that do not profit."

Why does the spirit of rebellion begin in pastors? Even if they are aware of the truth of the word, they act ignorant, and little by little the fear of God begins to wane in their lives.

To the pastors who are reading this book, I ask you to do a spiritual exercise: close your eyes for a minute and look inside. Review your heart and your conscience and evaluate if you have been preaching with the same conviction of sin as before. The spirit of rebellion is like leprosy, which begins to anesthetize our spiritual and moral feelings, when we realize it, we no longer consider anything as sin. Soon, it will no longer matter what they say about you, your family, or church.

For a time, I was a rebellious pastor, and I had a fear in my soul—a restlessness and a despair—because I wanted to be a hurricane of God again. But the shame of failure made me run and hide.

In the book of Proverbs 28:1 NKJV it says: "The wicked flee when no one pursues, But the righteous are bold as a lion.

I hid from the pastors when I walked the streets. One day, while walking through a shopping mall, I saw the President of the organization coming towards me. At the sight of him, my legs trembled with fear not knowing how I would be greeted. Good thing he didn't see me, and I could breathe a sigh of relief.

God is a merciful God, and he is always willing to forgive us if we repent so that we can be who we were created to be.

The fear that invades your being comes from hell, because the enemy of your soul makes you feel that way so that you don't recover what God has given you - your ministry. How will those who knew you as a pastor treat you? What will they say to you when they find you? Every kind of thought that comes to your mind to paralyze you wants you not to turn around and go back to the ministry. They say that the sheep (animal) is not very intelligent and only follows the voice of its shepherd when it hears him, and only follows in his footsteps when it sees him. This means that the pastor, to keep them in his fold (congregation), has to speak to their heart and lead them to green pastures with love.

This is what the Psalmist tells us in Psalm 23:1: NKJV "The Lord is my shepherd; I shall not want". Was David remembering when he was a shepherd? Out in the field he might lack food, but for his father's sheep there was pasture; water might be lacking, but the sheep were led to the still waters. That is, the father's sheep will always have what they need. This should be the concern of the good shepherd: that his sheep never lack for anything.

The good shepherd must not be interested in what the sheep can offer him. But there are shepherds who are more interested in what kind of wool they can get from the sheep than in providing care for them. In some places, wool refers to money. When the sheep has a lot of wool, then we can cut it; but when wool is scarce, therefore, we pay no attention to such sheep.

In the country where I am now, there are many shepherds who have left their fold and fled to other countries, because here there is a shortage of everything. Without food, or medicine, there is almost nothing here. But I wonder, "Would that be a reason to forsake the, Father's sheep?" The good shepherd should always be attentive to the needs of his sheep to show them where there are green pastures.

There is no better shepherd than Jesus Christ. To Him be all the glory and praise! Because He didn't run away from the cross, didn't want to escape the wicked soldiers, rather, He stood firm and allowed the cruel to take Him. He did not open his mouth and behaved like a mute sheep, suffering for our sins.

I have a question: "What did the shepherds do when there was a storm in the air?" I imagine they had to find a den - a safe place - to house their sheep. Perhaps, among the hills, there was a hiding place, in which the sheep would be safe and safe from the danger of the storm. Was there also a safe place for the shepherds?

If the sheep follow the voice of their shepherd, perhaps he would go into the pits first to see if there were any enemies, and his sheep would be safe. And the shepherd would be with them until the storm passed. Today, it's different. Shepherds have abandoned their sheep and they have sought, by themselves, where to hide, being lost, and without shepherds.

I personally heard from people who had been my sheep that I resigned from the ministry. Many did not know what to do. Even though the mission had sent another missionary in my place, it wasn't the same. And the church was gone in no time. Many went to the world, others sought other churches, but they were not well received. Anyway, I felt guilty for quite a while. If anyone who belonged to the church known as A Igreja da Carpa (the church tent), I ask for forgiveness for abandoning them.

The responsibility of being the pastor of a group of souls is great before God, because you need to learn to listen to the voice and instructions of the Holy Spirit. We are God's representatives on Earth, and we should be fearful in dealing with wounded sheep, because they all belong to the Father.

We are no better than anyone else. The difference is that we were chosen to lead a group of our Father's sheep, and it was He who was pleased to give them to us, for us to take care of, for the sake of the Gospel of Christ Jesus our Lord. Therefore, if you are called Bishop, Apostle, or Pastor, it is not because of your merit or because you are better than others, or more beautiful than others. Take away all your pride, for it is by the mercy and blood of Jesus, other than that, we are nothing and we have nothing to be proud of. The Apostle Paul says that the only thing he had to boast about was the cross of Christ.

8

FREE FOR YOUR MERCY

"Surely He shall deliver you from the snare of the fowler and from the perilous pestilence." Psalms 91:3 NKJV

I was returning from a Mission convention in Houston - Texas, and upon arriving at the local airport, I missed my flight to the interior of the country where I used to live, due to an electrical storm. The airline sent me to a hotel on the coast of the city.

It was five o'clock in the morning when the taxi came to me pick up and take me to the airport. The taxi driver kindly took my bags and he threw them into the trunk of the car, then opened the back door of the car for me, and I got in without a second thought. Next to the driver was another man who, immediately made me think something was wrong. I tried to open the car door, but I couldn't find the door latch, nor even the handle to lower the window. I soon realized that I was locked inside the car that was already speeding. I tried to negotiate with them and convince them to leave me somewhere. But they didn't answer me with even a word.

Instead of taking the road to the airport, the car started heading towards a very ugly neighborhood, and few people were walking around. Suddenly, the car stopped abruptly, and I tried to get out, but the man outside was much bigger and stronger than me.

The two men in the car started tying my hands and feet, covering my mouth with tape, and blindfolding me so that I couldn't see anything. With that, the only thing I could see was the impurity of my heart. Because I thought I would have little time to live, my whole story happened before my eyes, like a bad movie, with all my sins, disobedience, and mistakes. What I longed for most was a miracle of life, a new chance. So, I started crying out to God. In my despair, I told God that I would change my life, change my course, and become a saint.

I was stopped by three armed men. As I lay on the floor of the car, time felt like an eternity. All I knew was that the minutes passed very quickly. I already expected a shot to the head, which would be the end of the torture I was living. I felt that the car, which previously ran at a high speed, was now starting to run along an unpaved road and, therefore, it jumped a lot. This lasted a few minutes (perhaps ten), and we were back on the paved road again at great speed. The man in the back seat with me grabbed my shirt and lifted me up, saying, "If you say anything, we'll kill you right here."

It was at that moment that they began to cut the bonds from my hands, and to untie my feet and hands, threatening me with death. Again, they put me in the back seat of the car, and that's when I saw four national police officers with two motorcycles, one on each side of the vehicle, pointing their guns and shouting for them to stop, otherwise they would open fire. "Get out of the car with your hands in the air and throw yourself on the ground", was the order given. With nothing else to do, the four of us got out of the car and dropped to the ground. Immediately, I identified myself as kidnapped by that group. Then they lifted me up and set me apart from the others, who were still on the ground.

The officers gathered my suitcase and a guitar I was carrying with me, found my wallet and took me to the airport so I could catch my flight back home. The police that took me to the airport told me that the four policemen were talking near the entrance to the city dump, when they noticed a white taxi passing by at the same time and became suspicious, so they started the pursuit until they stopped the vehicle.

God had answered my prayers. It was a great relief to come out of this nightmare unscathed. It was a terrible anguish, but the moment I took the plane to my city, it felt like it was just a bad dream, because I had forgotten the promise I had made to God. The addiction to illicit sex had tied me hands and feet, the pleasures of the flesh held me prisoner and I returned to the same life as before.

The promises that had been made to God in my captivity had now, in a few hours, been forgotten. I believe I am not the only one who has made promises to God thinking I can deceive Him, forgetting that He knows all things. He had already been in my future and so knew that the words I said at the time of my despair were not sincere. God delivered me from death because his purpose in my life had not been fulfilled. There are people who make promises to get out of a bad season and then go back to doing whatever comes to mind. Do not think that you deceived God, for He knows that all these promises were empty, but still He delivered you from death and the abyss.

Maybe you've also told God a thousand times that you're going to change your life (stop lying, be faithful to your wife or husband), but when you realize it, you've fallen, again, into someone else's arms. Not to mention the "last drink", which was never the last. The fact is, you and I are hopelessly weak in ourselves, our flesh is stronger than our spirit, and when we realize it, we find ourselves in the same hole.

The Apostle Paul, in the book of Romans 7:19-20, says: "For the good that I will to do, I do not do; but the evil I will not to do, that I practice. 20 Now if I do what I will not to do, it is no longer I who do it, but sin that dwells in me."

These verses were written by someone we have as our teacher after Jesus. It was he who wrote letters to the churches, with instructions on how to live a holy life consecrated to God. But, in this account, it was as if Paul looked back into his interior and expressed himself in this way. He realized he wasn't perfect.

As long as we are alive in this body, we will constantly fight our human nature without rest. The same Paul said that our struggle is not against flesh or blood, but against our carnality. The only way to master our carnal impulses is to submit to the Spirit of the Lord daily, taking our ears, eyes and thoughts captive at the foot of the cross.

"How can a young man cleanse his way? By taking heed according to Your word." Psalm 119:9 NKJV

In the psalm above, David asks himself a question aloud and answers himself. He knew that when we keep the Word, we distance ourselves from the arrows of sin, and we do not grieve the heart of the heavenly Father. Regardless of age, we are all on the same path. If we detach ourselves from the word of God the enemy of our souls will make us easy prey for him, that was the reason Paul said he had to die to the world every day of his life. Making sin die in us every day is no easy task - believe me, it's harder than doing a hundred sit-ups daily. I, for example, exercise sporadically. When the belly is stretched out and the pants are already tight, that's when I decide I have to do something to alleviate the situation. But in the spiritual, we cannot act like this, rather, it is necessary to put on the armor of God every day, and be captives of Christ, to have the strength to walk with God.

9

THE DECEPTIVE HEART

"Deceitful is the heart, more than all things. And wicked, it is who may know him." Jeremiah 17:9 NKJV

Foolish is the person who walks around doing evil, knowing that this is not right in the eyes of God, and not even to human eyes. In fact, when you're overpowered by your carnal desires, the sin that surrounds you becomes a satanic force that invades your entire being, blocking your spiritual sensors and leading you astray from the father's path. It turns into something stronger than you that makes you walk in your own sinful way.

According to the word of God, the way of salvation is narrow and in order to walk through it we have to put off many things we drag from the world; few decide to enter it. For example: denying yourself and taking up your cross is a difficult discipline which only the brave do. Those who do not have self-control cannot do this. Why are there so many people asking us for prayer? Because they never prayed for themselves but prefer to live on the prayers of others. They are always spiritually weakened and never advance. They are anemic survivors of faith in Christ Jesus.

How did I preach, sing, pray, knowing I was wrong in the eyes of God?

There is a mechanism we use to convince ourselves that we are not harming anyone. And in case we prefer to look the other way, and no one warns us, we keep moving forward. That was the mechanism I used.

One afternoon, I remember being alone in my office, and my secretary had already gone home, when suddenly someone rang the doorbell - it was my assistant pastor. He was moved, crying, and facing my sin (until this moment, nothing had confronted me before). With great arrogance, I gave him a week to pack his bags and return to his city. Really, I wasn't willing to put the brakes on my rampant living. Lust had gotten me into the double life delusion, and that was how I walked.

I no longer cared about the ministry, but what I wanted was like a drug: every day, I needed a dose of illicit sex to fill the void of God in my life. When we don't make room for the Holy Spirit, He cannot convict us of sin and our minds are seared with guilt.

What is it that makes a man, or a woman, who has vowed before God to serve him in holiness, begin to deviate from all divine rules and fall? Many of us have heard of Catholic priests who have broken all the oaths they have taken before their superiors and we have excuses for them because they do not seek the Lord like we do. We can give them a thousand excuses, but they are just like us. If we are not under the authority of the Holy Spirit, we are pure carnality, just like them. If we let sin block our communion with God, we will lose all reverence, and holy things will begin to wane to such an extent that it no longer makes any difference between the saint and the worldly.

That's how it happened with the priest Eli. Little by little he allowed the most holy place to be stained by his spiritual blindness and contaminated by the sin of his children. Sin begins to creep in in a subtle way, like pornography: innocently, a person turns on the television in a hotel room and realizes that the last guest left it set on the channel that is showing an adult movie. They have the controller in their hands, but they freeze, their fingers freeze, and then they decide to watch "just a little bit" to see what will happen. But before you know it, they're already watching the second movie. Finally, they will still be able to excuse themself, saying that they were alone, no one saw them, and they even asked God for forgiveness. But this is a diabolical lie, for the seed has already been planted in that person's mind and subconscious. And sooner or later, they will return to that same filthy situation. The sin of the flesh becomes a chemical addition (illicit sex), which is only discharged with the immoral act itself. So, it is with those who use euphoric substances. For them to enter another dimension, they do what they can. To get money to buy drugs, they rob their own family members. All this in order to achieve what will satisfy their passion.

10
MY ADVICE TO YOU

"Where there is no counsel, the people fall; But in the multitude of counselors there is safety." Proverbs 11:14 NKJV

The best thing anyone can do is not travel alone for a long time. If you know that you will be staying in a hotel, but don't have your wife or husband, invite a friend to accompany you. Do not think you are stronger than you really are, because your sexual carnality is stronger. You are only master of those things that you can dominate and, unfortunately, many who are called Christians cannot dominate this area of their life. So don't fall apart but hold on to God to have complete victory.

I was very surprised to find that someone very known in my denomination was accused of looking at pornography while staying at a hotel He was there to attend a meeting of executive elders, but one of those who belonged to a local church raised the alarm, and he had to leave his pulpit for two years. Just because you are a Bishop, Apostle, or Presiding Pastor of a church does not mean that Satan will not attack your life. Rather, 1 Corintians 10.12 NKJV "Let him that is standing beware that he does not fall," said the Apostle Paul. In Romans 7:20, NKJV it also says, "But if I do what I do not want, it is no longer I who do it, but sin that dwells in me."

Paul was a great man of God who had struggles going on inside him (his mind). At that time, he didn't have a devilish television in his room that, simply by flicking his fingers, could bring whoever wanted to spend time with him.

In between mission services, I was also an Evangelist who preached in spiritual revival services. For days at a time, I had to preach in some churches about salvation, deliverance, and divine healing. But really, I don't know how I did it, because I was the one who needed all these things.

I remember one church in particular, located in the State of Iowa, that I arrived on a Wednesday to preach until the following Sunday. I opened my Bible and for hours I didn't know what I was going to say in the service. Without having a direction from God, because the one who was sick, empty and in need of healing for the soul was me, I cried: "Lord, have mercy on me! Don't make me ashamed."

That week was frustrating. Once you become addicted to pornography, it becomes the master of your mind. Then, even in the silence, it replays over and over again, activating the thoughts again. Silence makes it come even stronger. Maybe it's like an alcoholic or a smoker that it never stops satisfying the craving.

The Apostle Paul, in defending his ministry, in 2 Corinthians 10:5 NKJV says, Casting down arguments and every high thing that exalts itself against the knowledge of God, bringing every thought into captivity to the obedience of Chist.

Taking our thoughts captive is no easy task. Not letting our mind wander in any direction is very difficult. First, you need to acquire discipline and self-control.

Being disciplined in seeing only the things that suit you is not easy, especially for those who have already extinguished the fire of the Holy Spirit in their hearts. I would first turn on the television to watch a football game, or the news in the newspaper, but if I happened to be on a channel that showed something of lust, there I was. The internal struggles I had were very strong and unmeasured, because when I preached the word, I no longer talked about sins, much less lust.

I was especially afraid of going to small churches, as they always have a lot of prayer. I feared that God would use the sisters, who spend all their time praying, to reveal my sin. In particular, I remember going to one of these churches in southern Illinois, where an elderly woman came to me and said, "Thus says the Lord: My grace is still upon you, but you need to seek out My face". I confess that I was paralyzed, unable to take a step, thinking that God had told her what I was going through. I breathed a sigh of relief as she turned and disappeared from that place.

Living a double life is very stressful, it's the biggest pressure I've experienced in my entire life. Our nerves get to the point of exploding just thinking that at any moment someone could face us with the truth of our life, or the possibility of being unmasked in front of people who know us. All this took away my peace.

How nice it is to be able to lay your head on the pillow in peace and be free from any worries. It is tiring, often, not being able to sleep, because of the guilt of being a miserable sinner.

To you who are reading the lines of this book, and who are living such a life, I instruct you, today, in the name of Jesus, not to continue one day more in this state of life. For in this way you are destroying your spiritual life and your body. It is obvious that if you live in this practice of sin, your spiritual life is dead, and everything you do is mechanical, memorized.

Your physique will also suffer, because the nervous system makes your body not sleep well during the nights, which brings you fatigue, loss of energy, excessive worry, headache, in addition to diseases such as gastritis, which causes everything you eat to make you sick. The Bible is clear that the wage of sin is death, both spiritual and physical. I believe that one thing affects the other, because we are tripartite - body, soul, and spirit. In creating Adam, God molded his body and then breathed the breath of life. In this breath came the spirit - the place where your soul is hidden.

The Father's connection is perfect. If you have a pure mind, your spirit will be light and free from any oppression, which will give you physical energy to live better. If you exercise by running, or play sports, your physical body will feel good, as will your spirit. God has synchronized the three things to work in perfection whenever your soul is right with God.

11

THE WEIGHT OF SIN

"Therefore, we also, since we are surrounded by so great a cloud of witnesses, let us lay aside every weight, and the sin which so easily ensnares us, and let us run with endurance the race that is set before us" Hebrews 12:1 NKJV

To sin, momentarily, for a second of carelessness, is one thing, but sinning all the time knowing what you are doing is wrong before God and in the presence of all that are around you. It's an emotional disturbance without size, where you have no peace, and you have no strength to continue the path of your calling. Do not keep secretly anything in your life, for it will bring you bitterness of spirit and will take away your peace to eat or sleep. The remorse in your conscience will not give you peace of mind. Illicit sexual pleasure only lasts for a short time, but it leaves a lingering sadness in your spirit, in addition to a feeling of impurity that, no matter how much you bathe, you cannot cleanse your soul.

In 2 Samuel 12, king David got up one morning and, to his surprise, at his door was the prophet, Nathan. The scriptures don't give us many details, but I can already imagine that David suspected that God was not happy with the things that were happening in the palace. His sin was still hidden from men, but God had already seen it all.

And the story that the prophet Nathan told David was moving and sad, to the point that the king was indignant with the attitude of the rich man, not realizing that he was the unjust rich man in the story, who had all the women he wanted and yet, for the price of a life, he got another woman who was the wife of one of his soldiers.

Today, I am aware of all the damage I caused with my rebellion. I know that I have wounded many with words, and killed many in spirit, because I hardened my heart to the voice of the Holy Spirit.

Once again before God, without mentioning names, I want again to ask forgiveness from everyone I have hurt or mistreated, either with words or deeds. FORGIVE ME! If I caused you a pain in your heart and, therefore, you went into the world, only God knows the size of my regret.

To my former wife, I ask you for forgiveness. To my children, forgive me. To my church, which I pastored, I am sorry. And to my Lord and Savior Jesus, who has already forgiven me, thank you for your mercy and forgiveness. Thank you for having me home once again. I know I'm not perfect now, but I've become more prudent than before.

Time leaves a mark that shows us that the valley through which we have crossed has served to improve our relationship with God, and not to our death. The writer of the book of Hebrews, in Chapter 12 (the verse that heads this Chapter), talks about the weight of sin and the cloud of witnesses that are around us, watching our lives, whether for good or ill.

When you do good, that is, what is right before God and men, you will bring glory to our Father's name, and people who look at you will say that you are truly a child of God. Now, if you live a disastrous life, that same cloud of witnesses will say bad things about your God and generally put all evangelicals in the same bag. Therefore, if an evangelical acts like a thief, then everyone will be labeled a thief. People will always see things by the color white or black. Therefore, the Christian must walk in the light to shine the glory of God.

When I pastored, I always told my parishioners that if they can't model a Christian life, then don't say they are a Christian. In that case, it is better to say that you are a church sympathizer, or that you like gospel music, than to say that you are evangelical. That way when you sin, others will not generalize evangelicals, but will use your personal name. This is better for God, for the church and for yourself, because if you're just another one on the bench, you won't say anything, but when you identify yourself as God's church, things take different proportions.

12

BE HUMBLE

_____

"The fear of the Lord is the instruction of wisdom, and before honor is humility."
Proverbs 15:33 NKJV

Mom always said that it's the pain that teaches us to moan, that makes you value medicine, which can calm your anguish. I never wanted to seek the help that was within my reach. I decided that I could heal myself, with my common sense whenever I wanted - that's what I said to myself.

On one occasion, the apostle Paul said that he carried in his body the marks of Christ - marks for obedience to God, for his straight life. But some people bear other marks. The ones I have, for example, are still due to my disobedience to God. I have nothing to boast about except in the redeeming blood of Jesus.

Friend and brother who is reading these pages, do not think that you are capable of overcoming this addiction with your own strength. Rather, seek the face of God, and also the help of someone you trust who is at a higher spiritual level than you (like your pastor). And stop swimming in the turbulent waters of this sinful sea that leads you to perdition.

I will give you the sequence of how carnal addictions usually start: 1) Restricted movies; 2) Masturbation; 3) Pornographic films; 4) finally, illicit sex. The bible says that an abyss calls another abyss, just as Seoul is insatiable, so is the sin of the flesh: the more you see, the more your flesh desires. The flesh is insatiable and sinful in the extreme and can fall over and over again.

Everything I'm describing in this book is what I've been through. My wish is that you do not get to the point of addiction that I did. In the name of Jesus, renounce these things, take possession of spiritual authority, and subject your body, making it obey your spirit. I've heard of people who, after having fallen, started walking with women from the streets. But thank God that I was freed, by his mercy, before I got to this situation.

13

BREAK THE ADDICTION

_____

"And if your foot causes you to sin, cut it off. It is better for you to enter life lame, rather than having two feet, to be cast into hell, into the fire that shall never be quenched." Mark 9:45 NKJV

Once again, I want to ask you friend, husband, apostle, pastor, evangelist, and teachers of the word: how much longer will you play with sin in secret? In all my years of ministry, I have never had such passion and compassion for many who are suffering from this evil in silence. You can't let anyone know, not even your wife. The devil says you have lost credibility with those who believe you to be holy. What will others say about you?

I know there are thousands of men and women who are fighting in secret, just as I fought years ago. They are imprisoned by their desires, but also possess a heart that wants to give itself to the service of God. This fight is strong and often, when ministering, a sense of guilt wears them out and does not allow them to have true freedom to preach with the full anointing of God.

In the country where I was a missionary, I had a friend who was the pastor of a beautiful church, which had many members. Despite the distance, he came to preach at mine and I at his. So, we decided to start a ministry for men, which we called Men of Valor.

We began to travel many places together, preaching to men, believers, and non-believers, teaching them how to treat their wives. These meetings took place on Fridays and Saturdays, and on Sundays we ended up with all the families together. In these meetings I was often surprised to see how 90% of the men went to the altar to pray, in addition to pastors who also had the courage to ask for prayers. And we ministered to these needy people.

My friend and I were safe from all the things we saw and heard. We knew that our struggle was spiritual. But as much as I listened to the stumbling of others, it seemed that my mind didn't register that I was in greatest need of deliverance. We need to understand that even though our soul came from heaven and entered our body, this body is sinful and full of carnal habits, without the help of the Holy Spirit.

Our ministry ended suddenly, without a word of farewell. We were in the middle of a conference, in a city far from home. There was a big turnout that Sunday night, where all the families were gathered to close the conference. That's when someone approached me with a message from my friend, saying that he was returning to his city and that I was in charge of closing the last meeting. I confess that I was confused, not knowing what to think. As my friend was a great speaker, he was always the one who closed the conferences.

To this day I don't know what actually happened to my friend. He left the country and left behind great sadness of people who genuinely loved him. I never judged him for making that decision, but I always had a question in my mind: what led him to make that decision?

Please, dear reader, if by chance something similar has happened to you, and in the illusion of your mind, someone is making you make a drastic decision like this, I ask you not to. Do not abandon your home or your church. It's not worth acting like that, because later on, you will surely regret it. But choose to be faithful to God, your wife and your calling. What you have is more precious than anything else that comes from the opposite side of what God has given you.

14

ESCAPE THE PLOT OF SIN

"and that they may come to their senses and escape the snare of the devil, having been taken captive by him to do his will" Timothy 2:26 NKJV

For me, one of the first characters in the Bible who shows to be filled with the Holy Spirit is young Joseph. He was far from his homeland and from the eyes of his father, Jacob. But he was also more aware of the purpose of God in his life that would only come true if he escaped illicit sex. The only one that gives you the strength to escape the clutches of a seducing woman is the Holy Spirit, and this evidence is found in a young man of puberty age.

The Bible doesn't tell us her name, we only know her as Potiphar's wife. However, it could have been any other woman, of any skin color, member of any church, or even a non-believer. We don't know how she is, but we know what she is called: "Killer" of God's dreams for your life.

Pastors, another advice I give you is not to give an audience to women who are alone unless your wife is with you. Don't give anyone a ride, not even the lowliest granny in town, because it can often start to bring up bad thoughts.

It was not David's first eye contact with Bathsheba that led to his adultery, but the act of standing in the same place, contemplating her beauty. If he had gone where he was supposed to be, in the war, maybe he wouldn't have gotten into so much trouble.

Another piece of advice, this time, for all of us, is that we don't look where we shouldn't look, so as not to affect our spirit, because we don't know when to stop. So don't tempt your flesh, rather be wise. If your weakness is alcohol, don't go to any party where there will be alcoholic drinks and don't walk past a liquor store. If your problem is sexual, don't walk where there will be people offering sexual favors on the street. Don't increase the size of your struggle, or make it heavier than it already is, and then God will give you victory.

15

THE SHAME OF SIN

"They have all turned aside, they have together become corrupt; There is none who does good, No, not one." Psalms 14:3 NKJV

After my spiritual failure, I was very worried about what people would say about me. My sensitivity had risen to a very high level. I knew it did not matter how much good I might have done before my spiritual slip, no one could say anything good about me.

The woman who was brought into the presence of Jesus, being caught in the act, was caught in her sin, and no one in the crowd raised his hand and said, "Jesus, let's give her an opportunity to repent!", or "Let's have a little mercy on her." Everyone held stones in their hands - stones of guilt, of hatred and of death. The only who had no stone in his hands was Jesus. His arms were open to hug her and help her. "Go and sin no more", was the Master's order. He didn't say, "You can't sing in the choir," or "You can't speak of my name." He simply ordered her not to sin anymore.

By that, I don't mean that I could expect anything other than the repudiation of my friends and the punishment of writing a letter renouncing my credentials.

Don't expect them to throw roses your way. For a long time, I walked around dodging stones of condemnation and being pointed out as a great confessed sinner. If you think like this: "I have it hidden and nothing is known yet", or, "I can hold on a little longer", confess your transgressions and your sin will be forgiven. Don't delay any longer. Because it will also affect your physical body, as your spirit is weakened.

How many of us have had heart attacks? How many have psyche problems? How many in depression? Usually, we blame the work, or the stress of the ministry, but if we dig a little, maybe it's not those cases, but something hidden, unconfessed before God, can bring about such things.

Please, I'm not generalizing that all men and women of God have hidden sins in their lives and get sick because of it. But our body is a machine, created by a perfect God, that wears out and fails. I, for example, two years ago suffered three heart attacks after preaching in a Sunday service at my church. Doctors attribute this event to many other physical aspects that I suffer, but only I know what I went through for a while, not being able to sleep and without peace of mind that led to my heart attack.

Finally, I want to tell you that you are not alone. God is with you to help you. He loves you and understands you. But He also expects you to make a firm decision to seek His face, to obtain mercy. And one more thing: I sympathize with your story, and I will pray for you as it is my wish that you too be free, in Jesus's name.

Printed in the United States
by Baker & Taylor Publisher Services